THE LION
Bible *for* Me

Retold by
Christina Goodings
Illustrated by
Emily Bolam

LION
CHILDREN'S

Text by Christina Goodings
Illustrations copyright © 2012 Emily Bolam
This edition copyright © 2012 Lion Hudson

The moral rights of the author and illustrator
have been asserted

A Lion Children's Book
an imprint of
Lion Hudson plc
Wilkinson House, Jordan Hill Road,
Oxford OX2 8DR, England
www.lionhudson.com
ISBN 978 0 7459 6264 1

First edition 2012
10 9 8 7 6 5 4 3 2 1 0

Acknowledgments
The Lord's Prayer (on page 62) as it appears in *Common Worship: Services
and Prayers for the Church of England* (Church House Publishing, 2000)
is copyright © The English Language Liturgical Consultation and is
reproduced by permission of the publisher.

A catalogue record for this book is available
from the British Library

Typeset in 14/19 Goudy Old Style
Printed in China December 2011 (manufacturer LH17)

Distributed by:
UK: Marston Book Services Ltd, PO Box 269, Abingdon, Oxon OX14 4YN
USA: Trafalgar Square Publishing, 814 N Franklin Street, Chicago, IL
60610
USA Christian Market: Kregel Publications, PO Box 2607, Grand Rapids,
MI 49501

About the Bible

The Bible is a wonderful collection of stories
and sayings from long ago.

It tells of how the world came to be the way it is.

It tells of people's longing to do what is good
and right: to be friends of God.

It tells of times when people got things right
and times when they got things wrong.

It tells of Jesus, who told people what to do
to live as God's friends, now and always.

In the beginning

Once there was only dark.

God spoke: "Let there be light." At once it shone – like fire, like diamonds.

God made the wide blue sky and the deep green sea. God made the good brown earth, from which seeds uncurled and reached up high.

God made golden sun, the silver moon, and stars for the night.

God made the fish and the birds and every kind of animal: the great and the small, the fierce and the funny.

Then God made people. "This world is your lovely home," said God. "Please take care of it."

The making was done: it was time for a day of rest.

The garden of Eden

God planted a garden in Eden: it was a paradise home for Adam and Eve.

"You can eat from any of these trees," said God, "except the one in the middle. Its fruit will harm you."

When Eve was alone, a snake slithered up. "That's untrue," it hissed. "That fruit will make you wise."

Eve picked the fruit and shared it with Adam. At once, they felt ashamed. When God came to talk with them, they hid.

"Now you must leave paradise," said God. "Beyond the garden, life will be very hard."

And so it was. Worst of all, the friendship between God and people was spoiled.

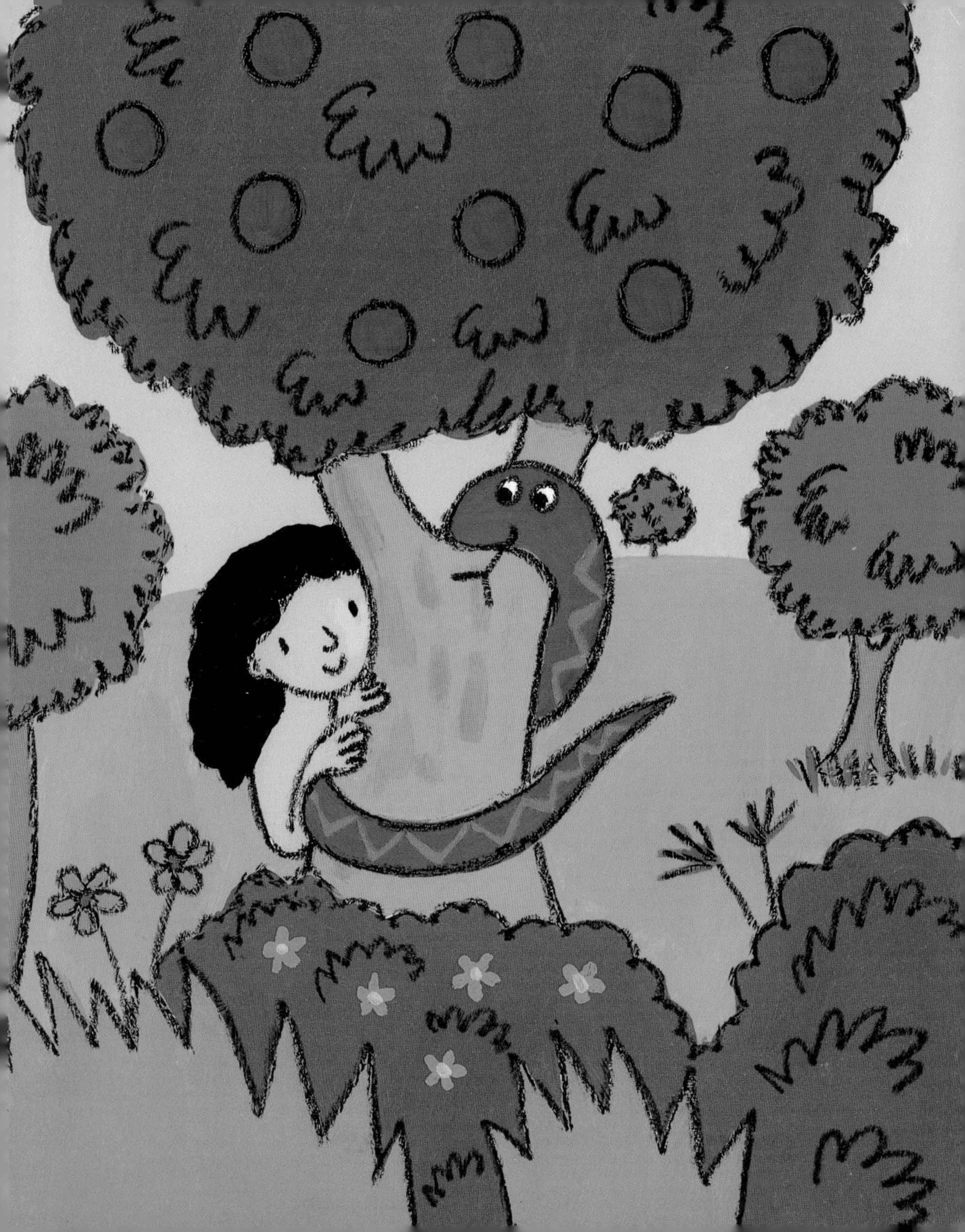

Noah and the flood

People grew wicked. Only Noah was good.

"I want you to build an ark," said God to
Noah. "Take on board your family and two
of every animal. I am going to send a flood."

Noah did as God asked. Then came the rain.
The ark floated all alone on a great grey flood.

After many days, the rain stopped. Slowly the
flood ebbed away.

"Come out of the ark," said God to Noah.
"It's time to start the world again.

"Look: there is a rainbow. It is my promise
to you that there will be summer and winter,
seedtime and harvest for ever."

Abraham and the night sky

It was night-time. Abraham sat outside his tent. He could hear his sheep and goats and cattle munching grass nearby.

"I am a wealthy herdsman," he said. "I have made my home in this good land of Canaan.

"But my wife Sarah and I have no son."

Then God spoke, quietly and clearly. "Try to count the stars, Abraham. You will have a son, and your children's children will be as many as that.

"Your family will bring my blessing to the world."

One day, God's promise came true. Abraham and Sarah named their son "Isaac", and the name means "laughter".

Joseph and his brothers

Joseph was one of the grandsons of Isaac; he was also the favourite of his father Jacob, who gave him a beautiful coat.

Joseph's ten elder brothers were jealous. One day, they sold him to be a slave in Egypt. They told Jacob that animals had eaten him.

God took care of Joseph. He helped the young slave explain dreams. Even the king was impressed. Joseph became very important.

Years passed. The harvests failed, and Joseph's ten brothers came to Egypt begging to buy food. Joseph forgave them for what they had done.

"Come to Egypt to live," he said. "There is food for all of you... and my father... and my littlest brother Benjamin too."

So they came: the people of Israel.

The baby in the basket

Years passed. Egypt had a new king. He did not like the people of Israel.

"Make them slaves," he ordered. "Drown their baby boys."

A mother made a basket that would float. She put her baby boy inside and hid it among the reeds by the river.

Her daughter Miriam watched as the Egyptian princess came to bathe. She saw the princess find her brother.

"The little darling! I shall make him mine," the princess said. "I shall name him 'Moses'."

Miriam stepped near. "I know someone who can look after him," she said.

She went to get her mother. "Please keep little Moses safe for me," said the princess.

Out of Egypt

Moses grew up as a prince in Egypt. Even so, he knew he was one of the people of Israel. He was angry that his people were slaves.

One day, God spoke. "Take the people of Israel to Canaan," said God. "That will be their home."

But slaves were useful to the king of Egypt. "They can't leave," he told Moses.

Then there were all kinds of disasters: bad weather, swarms of insects, and worse. The king saw they were warnings from God. "Oh, take your people away," he told Moses.

God made a path through the Red Sea to help the people walk to freedom.

The promise

Between Egypt and Canaan lay the wilderness of Sinai.

The people of Israel lived there as nomads for forty years.

God helped them find water.

God provided quails and manna for them to eat.

God told Moses the laws they must obey: laws that would help them know what is right and good.

They must love God with all their heart and mind and soul and strength.

They must love other people as much as they loved themselves.

"This is the promise," Moses explained. "If you keep these laws, God will be your God. You will be God's people, and God will do good things for you."

Joshua and the walls of Jericho

Moses grew old. He chose Joshua to be the next leader.

"Be sure to keep my laws," God told him. "Then everything you do will turn out right."

Joshua led the people into Canaan. The first job was to capture Jericho.

Once a day, for six days, Joshua and the people marched around the city. "Ram-pah-pah-paah," went the trumpets. The soldiers of Jericho watched from the walls.

On the seventh day, Joshua and the people marched around seven times. "Ram-pah-pah-paaaaah!" went the trumpets. The people shouted. The walls of Jericho fell down.

God helped Joshua win the victory.

Gideon defends his people

The people of Israel made Canaan their home; but enemies from all around came plundering.

They needed champions to defend them.

Young Gideon was just a farmer. He was scared of the raiders who came to steal harvest crops.

"With my help, you will be a champion," said God.

So Gideon chose 300 brave fighters. They went and hid around the raiders' camp. Each had a trumpet and a blazing torch hidden in a jar.

In the dark of night, Gideon gave the sign. The men blew the trumpets. "Ram-pah-pah-paah."

They smashed the jars and held the blazing torches high.

The raiders panicked and ran away.

Ruth's new family

"Ooh," said Ruth. "My back is sore from bending to gather barley.

"But look how much I have."

She took it to her mother-in-law, Naomi. She and Naomi had no family but each other. They were very poor.

"Farmer Boaz was kind," Ruth explained. "He told his workers to leave lots of barley for us."

Naomi smiled. "I think he likes you," she said, "and no wonder: he can see how good you are to me.

"Listen: I have an idea."

The idea was that Ruth would ask Boaz to marry her.

Boaz agreed. Soon the family was Boaz and Ruth, their baby Obed... and proud grandmother Naomi.

Samuel hears a voice

There was a place of worship at Shiloh. The priest in charge was Eli. He was delighted to have a young helper named Samuel.

One of Samuel's jobs was to keep the lamps burning. He often slept near the great gold lamp stand.

One night he heard someone calling. He thought it was Eli... but it wasn't.

Three times Samuel heard the voice and three times he ran to Eli. "Next time," said Eli, "simply tell God you are listening."

God told Samuel that he would grow up to be the people's wise leader. For many years, Samuel helped people obey God's laws.

David and Goliath

Samuel was growing older. The people's enemies were getting bolder.

"Choose a king for us," the people cried.

With God's help, Samuel chose Saul. He was handsome and brave. Even so, neither he nor his soldiers dared fight the Philistine champion, Goliath.

David was a shepherd boy from Bethlehem. In fact, he was the great-grandson of Ruth.

"I can fight bears and lions to stop them taking my sheep," he said. "I'll fight Goliath."

He took his sling and five small stones and went to meet Goliath. "God will help me beat you!" he cried.

He slung his stone and Goliath fell down. The Philistines ran.

Everyone cheered for David.

Solomon's golden temple

David was a great warrior. He defeated all the people's enemies and became king. He built the city of Jerusalem on a hill.

"I want to build a new place of worship here: a beautiful temple," he declared. "It will be a home for the golden box in which we have kept God's laws safe since the time of Moses."

David made the plan, and his son Solomon arranged the building.

When it was done, there was a great celebration.

Solomon said a prayer: "O God, hear our prayers when we face this place and pray. In your home in heaven, hear us and forgive us."

Elijah and the fire

After Solomon, the people quarrelled. The one kingdom became two.

The people in the northern kingdom of Israel began to forget God's laws. One of their kings, Ahab, worshipped other gods.

Elijah gave him a warning.

"Because of your wickedness," he said, "God will send no rain."

The land dried up; the harvests failed. Ahab had to agree to what Elijah asked for next.

"Tell your priests to build a fire for your gods."

They did so.

"Now ask those gods to set it ablaze."

The priests asked, but nothing happened.

So Elijah built a fire. He said a prayer.

At once, God sent a fiery blaze from heaven.

Not long after, the rain came.

Jonah

One day, God came and spoke to Jonah.

"Go to Nineveh," said God. "Tell the people to change their wicked ways... or I will punish them."

Jonah frowned. "They deserve to be punished," he said to himself. He ran to the sea and got on a boat. It was bound for far away.

God sent a storm. Jonah was thrown overboard. A great sea creature came and swallowed him up.

"Help me, God," Jonah prayed. "I will do as you want."

The creature threw Jonah up on shore. Jonah hurried to Nineveh. "Change your wicked ways," he cried.

And they did: the king, the people, the children.

"I want to love and forgive everyone," said God.

Hezekiah trusts in God

To the north of the land of Israel lay Assyria and its great city of Nineveh.

The Assyrian army was fierce. First they defeated the kingdom of Israel. Then they marched to the southern kingdom of Judah and captured one city after another.

In Jerusalem, King Hezekiah grew afraid. He went to Isaiah, who was a man of God.

"Don't be frightened," said Isaiah. "When the Assyrians are cruel to us, our God is not pleased. God will defend us."

The Assyrian army was camped outside Jerusalem, but Hezekiah trusted in God.

Suddenly disease struck the Assyrian army. They went home without a fight. Jerusalem was safe.

The peaceable kingdom

Isaiah was always faithful to God. He knew that his people had not been so obedient. That was why the Assyrians had been able to win so many victories. Even so, Isaiah was sure that the kingdom that David had begun would be great again.

"One day, there will be a new king," said Isaiah. "God will make him wise and good. His kingdom will be at peace.

"Wolves and sheep will live together, and leopards with goats.

"Calves will feed with lions, and cows with bears.

"Little children will take care of them, and snakes will do no harm.

"Everyone will see that God alone is great and good."

Good King Josiah

Josiah was Hezekiah's great-grandson. He always tried to keep God's laws.

While he was king, the Temple in Jerusalem needed repairs. The builders found a long-forgotten copy of the book of God's laws. The priest took it to Josiah and read it aloud to him.

Josiah was dismayed at what he heard. "There are so many things God told us to do that we have not done," he cried. "We must put things right at once."

Josiah ordered the people to obey God's laws again. They celebrated a great festival – Passover. It was a time to remember that once they had been slaves in Egypt.

It was a time to give thanks to the God who sets people free.

Jerusalem in ruins

In the time of Josiah, the people in his kingdom knew they must obey God.

But after Josiah came other kings, and they forgot to be faithful.

A new enemy made war: King Nebuchadnezzar of Babylon, who wanted to be the ruler of everywhere. His armies defeated Jerusalem. They burned down the Temple. They took some people away from their home to live in Babylon.

In the ruined city, people sat and cried. They had no homes, no food. Everything had gone wrong.

Yet hope returned when they remembered one thing:

God's love and mercy are for ever – fresh as the morning, sure as the sunrise.

The fiery furnace

Among the people who went from Jerusalem to Babylon were three young men: Shadrach, Meshach, and Abednego. They were good and wise.

Then King Nebuchadnezzar had a golden statue made. Everyone went to see it.

"When the music plays," said the herald, "you must bow down."

The music played, but Shadrach, Meshach, and Abednego did not bow down. "We worship our God alone," they said.

King Nebuchadnezzar flew into a rage. "Throw them into a burning fiery furnace," he cried.

Into the flames went the three young men. God sent an angel to keep them safe.

When the king saw, he was scared. "Bring them out," he cried. "Their God is amazing."

Daniel and the lions

Daniel was loyal to the kings in Babylon; but every day he looked in the direction of Jerusalem and said his prayers.

When Darius became king, he gave Daniel the top job. That made other people jealous.

They went to Darius. "Your Majesty, you are great and wonderful," they said. "People should trust in you alone.

"You have made a law that no one should say prayers to anyone but you.

"But that Daniel... he says prayers to his God."

The law was the law. For saying his prayers, Daniel was thrown to the lions.

God sent an angel to keep Daniel safe.

"Bring Daniel out," said Darius. "It is clear that his God is the greatest of them all."

Home again

When Cyrus became king, he gave a new order.
All the peoples who had been forced to live
in Babylon could go home. That included the
Jews, whose home city was Jerusalem.

Many returned with high hopes.

It was hard work building their homes.

It was hard work building the Temple, and
it was not nearly as grand as the one that had
been burned down. It was hard work building
the walls to keep their city safe.

At last the work was done. There was a festival
of celebration.

A man of God named Zechariah gave words
of hope:

"One day, God will send a new king – a king
of peace."

The baby in the manger

An angel told Mary she would have a baby:
God's own Son.

An angel told Joseph to take care of Mary and
her child.

On the night Mary's baby was born, they were far
from home, in Bethlehem. There was no room in
the inn, so their shelter was a stable.

Out on the hills, shepherds were watching their
sheep. An angel appeared.

"Good news," said the angel. "Tonight, in
Bethlehem, God's chosen king has been born.
He will save the world from all that has gone
wrong.

"Go – you will find him wrapped in swaddling
clothes and lying in a manger."

The shepherds went and found Mary and Joseph
and little baby Jesus.

The wise men and the star

In lands to the east, wise men saw a bright new star. "It is a sign," they said. "A king has been born to the Jews."

They followed the star. After many miles they reached Jerusalem.

King Herod listened to the men. Their news upset him. His job was to make sure that everyone obeyed the Roman emperor. A real king meant trouble.

"What do you know about a king of the Jews?" he asked his advisers.

"God's chosen king will one day be born in Bethlehem," they said.

Herod sent the wise men to Bethlehem. The star lit their way to Jesus.

They brought their gifts: gold, frankincense, and myrrh.

Jesus grows up

Jesus grew up in Nazareth. From Joseph, he learned to be a carpenter. At school, he learned about his Jewish faith.

When Jesus was twelve, he went to Jerusalem for the Passover festival: to give thanks to the God who sets people free. Jesus went with his parents and a crowd from Nazareth. After the days of celebration, everyone started out for home.

Except for Jesus.

When Mary found out, she and her husband hurried back to Jerusalem.

At long last they found Jesus. He was in the Temple, talking with the wisest teachers of the Jewish faith.

"Why did you worry?" Jesus asked his mother. "Didn't you know I would be in my Father God's house?"

Then he went home with them, and grew up a good and obedient son.

Jesus is baptized

Jesus had a cousin named John. He looked like a man of God from olden days, with his uncut hair and his rough cloak. He lived in the wild country, eating simple food.

Everyone talked about his preaching.

"Turn away from wrongdoing," he called out to those who came to listen. "Let me baptize you in the river to show you are making a clean start. God will forgive you."

One day, Jesus came and asked to be baptized. As John lifted Jesus up out of the water, God's Holy Spirit settled on him in the form of a dove. A voice spoke from heaven: "You are my own dear Son; I am pleased with you."

Jesus and the fishermen

Jesus' baptism marked a new beginning. He did not let himself be tempted to choose an easy life. He was determined to do what God wanted.

He began preaching – in Nazareth and in the other towns of Galilee.

"I have good news," he told people. "It is time for God's kingdom... and you can be part of it. Turn away from wrongdoing and live as God wants."

Down by the shore of Lake Galilee were some fishermen: Simon Peter and Andrew, James and John.

"Come and help me gather people into God's kingdom," said Jesus.

The fishermen left their nets and followed Jesus.

How to be friends with God

Crowds came to listen to what Jesus had to say.

"Do you want to live as God wants?" he asked. "Then God will help you and bless you.

"You have heard the saying, 'Love your friends, hate your enemies.'

"I am telling you to love your enemies as well. Even bad people are good to the people who are good to them.

"Remember that God sends the sun and the rain to good and bad people alike. Remember to show kindness to good and bad people alike.

"That is how to be friends with God."

How to pray

"When you pray," said Jesus, "go to your room and close the door. Only your Father God will see you, and God will listen to you.

"Don't say long prayers. God already knows what you need. Say this:

> "Our Father in heaven,
> hallowed be your name,
> your kingdom come,
> your will be done,
> on earth as in heaven.
> Give us today our daily bread.
> Forgive us our sins
> as we forgive those who sin against us.
> Lead us not into temptation
> but deliver us from evil."

What really matters

"Make it your aim," said Jesus, "to live as a friend of God.

"Don't worry about having lots of things. They don't last for ever anyway. While you have them, you'll worry about someone stealing them.

"Look at the birds. They don't sow seeds. They don't gather a harvest. Yet God provides them with the food they need.

"Look at the wild flowers. They don't stitch and sew. Yet God clothes them in lovely petals – lovelier by far than any royal robes.

"Seek to be part of God's kingdom. God knows what you need, and God will take care of you."

The story of two houses

"Listen to my teaching," Jesus told the crowds. "Listen – and remember to obey.

"If you do, you are like the person who built a house high on a rock. The rain came down, the flood rose up, and the wind blew and blew. The house was safe through the fiercest storm.

"What if you listen to my words but forget to obey them? Then you are like the person who built a house on the sand by the river. The rain came down, the flood rose up, and the wind blew and blew. The house on the sand fell flat.

"What a crash!"

The hole in the roof

Jesus did not only talk about God. He showed God's love by healing those who were sick.

One day, Jesus was inside a house. People had come from far and wide to listen to him. When four men arrived, carrying a friend who could not walk, they could not get near the door.

Then they had an idea. They hurried up the outside stairs onto the flat roof. They made a hole in the roof and let their friend down on ropes – right in front of Jesus.

He looked up and saw the men, eager and hopeful.

He looked at their friend. "God forgives you," he said.

His words astonished some of the listeners, but then they saw what happened next.

"Get up and walk," said Jesus.

The man danced outside: he was healed.

Jairus and his daughter

Jairus was worried.

He had watched and waited as the boat carrying Jesus had sailed into harbour. He had elbowed and pushed through the crowd to get close to Jesus. He had pleaded with him to come and heal his daughter.

Jesus had said yes – but it was taking too long to get to the house.

Then a messenger arrived. "I'm sorry," he said, in a loud whisper. "Your little girl has just died."

"Don't worry," said Jesus. He went with Jairus to the house.

He went to the room where the girl lay still and pale. He took her hand and said, "Little girl, please get up."

At once she sat up. Jesus had brought her to life.

The lost sheep

"Anyone can be part of God's kingdom," said Jesus. "God is ready to forgive."

There were many who disagreed. So Jesus told a story.

"A man had a hundred sheep. One went missing.

"He left the ninety-nine safe in the pasture and started out to find the one that was lost. He didn't mind the stony path or the thorny bushes.

"He kept on looking until he found his sheep. Gently he picked it up and carried it home.

" 'We must celebrate,' he said to his friends. 'I have found the one sheep that was lost.'

"God is like that shepherd," said Jesus. "God is happy when the one who has lost their way is brought safely into the kingdom."

The forgiving father

Jesus told this story to show what God is like.

"A man had two sons. The elder worked hard on the farm. The younger had plans of his own.

"He demanded money from his father. Then he went to a city far away. He spent his money as if it would never run out.

"But hard times came. The son had to get a job, minding pigs.

" 'I'd be better off at home,' he sighed. 'I shall go and say I'm sorry.'

"He walked the long miles. He still had a way to go when his father came running.

" 'Welcome,' his father said.

" 'I'm sorry...' began the son.

" 'None of that!' laughed the father. 'It's time for a party. I thought I had lost you... but here you are alive and well.' "

The Good Samaritan

God's laws told people to love others. What did that mean?

Jesus told a story.

"A man was going from Jerusalem to Jericho. Thieves came and robbed him. They left him for dead in the road.

"A Temple priest came along. He saw the man, then hurried by on the other side.

"A Temple helper came along. He saw the man and came to look. Then he hurried away.

"A Samaritan came by – and Samaritans don't even worship in the Temple. He saw the man in the road. He went and bandaged his wounds. Then he took him to an inn and made sure he would be cared for until he was well.

"So who showed love to the man?" asked Jesus. "You decide."

The storm on the lake

Jesus often went by boat to different towns on the shore of Lake Galilee.

One evening, after a busy day, Jesus climbed aboard and lay down to sleep. His friends sailed the boat out onto the lake.

Suddenly a storm blew up. The wind howled. The waves crashed. The boat began to fill with water.

"Wake up, Jesus," his friends cried. "Don't you care that we might drown?"

Jesus stood up in the boat. "Hush," he said to the wind. "Lie down," he said to the waves.

At once the lake was calm.

His friends whispered among themselves, "Who can Jesus be? Even the wind and waves obey him."

A feast for five thousand

One day, a great crowd came to Jesus. They had heard of his miracles of healing and wanted to see for themselves.

"We should feed them," said Jesus to his friends. "Where can we get food?"

"It would cost a fortune to feed this many!" came the reply.

Another of the friends spoke up: "There is a boy here who has five loaves and two fish. It's not enough for a crowd."

"Ask the people to sit down," said Jesus.

When everyone was seated, Jesus took the food and said a prayer of thanks. He gave it to his friends to share with the crowd.

By a miracle, there was enough for everyone.

Jesus and the children

One day, some people brought their little children to Jesus.

First they had to get past his chosen followers. "Can we ask Jesus to say a blessing prayer for our little ones?" they asked.

"Our master is very busy," the men scolded. "He has important things to do... and important people to see."

Jesus heard what they said. "Bring the children over to me," he called cheerfully. "No one should try to stop them.

"The kingdom of God belongs to children like these.

"Anyone who wants to be part of the kingdom must have the simple trust of a child."

Jesus rides to Jerusalem

Jesus spent three years preaching and teaching.
The wise things he said and the miracles he worked
got people thinking: was he the king God had
promised to send?

One day, Jesus went to Jerusalem for the Passover
festival: to give thanks to the God who sets people
free. There were crowds of people going there for
the same reason.

They saw Jesus, riding on a donkey.

"God bless the king," shouted someone. Then
lots of people joined in. They cut branches from
palm trees and waved them like flags.

They began to hope: perhaps Jesus was going to
do something amazing to set their people free.

Trouble

Not everyone in Jerusalem was pleased to see Jesus.

"His preaching has got us worried," muttered the teachers of the faith. "Too much about love, not enough about the Law."

"And he's wrong to let the people treat him as God's chosen king."

The Temple priests were angry too. "He came into the courtyard and threw out everyone who had a market stall," they complained. "He said the Temple was meant to be a house of prayer. What does he expect at festival time?"

They began to plot together to get rid of Jesus. Then one of Jesus' own followers, Judas Iscariot, came in secret and said he would help them.

The last supper

It was Passover time. Jesus and his chosen followers gathered to share the festival meal: to give thanks to the God who sets people free.

"I'm so glad to share this meal with you all before the trouble begins," said Jesus. "It will have a new meaning in the kingdom of God."

He took a piece of bread, broke it, and shared it among them. "This is my body, which is given for you," he said. "Do this in memory of me."

He took the cup of wine and passed it to them to share. "This cup is God's new promise – signed and sealed with my blood.

"Whenever you drink it, do so in memory of me."

Jesus forgives

After the supper, Jesus and his followers went to an olive grove. Jesus went away to say prayers.

Judas Iscariot had slipped away. He came later to where they all were – bringing armed men. They took Jesus away to a night-time meeting of the priests and teachers.

"You're a troublemaker," they said. "Worse, you insult God by letting people think you're his chosen king. You are guilty."

They took Jesus to the Roman governor, Pontius Pilate. "You must punish this Jesus," they said, "or there'll be trouble."

Pilate gave the order. His soldiers put Jesus to death, nailed to a cross.

From the cross Jesus looked at those who had wronged him: "Father God, forgive them," he said.

The first Easter

Jesus died on the cross. Some friends came and took his body to a tomb. It was sunset: the weekly day of rest was beginning. They rolled the stone door shut and hurried home.

The day of rest came and went. Very early on the next morning, some women went back to the tomb to say a last goodbye.

To their dismay, the stone door was rolled open. Jesus' body was gone.

They stood there wondering what had happened. Two angels in shining cloths appeared. "Why are you looking among the dead for one who is alive?" asked the angels.

"Jesus is not here: he is risen."

Good news

The news about Jesus began to spread among his followers.

"Can he really be alive?"

"He really is! We've seen him!"

The risen Jesus told his followers what they must do: "Tell the world the things I told you about God's love and forgiveness. Tell them that they can be set free from wrongdoing and belong to God's kingdom.

"God will send his Spirit to help you."

Not long after, Jesus said goodbye and was taken up to heaven.

Ten days after that came a harvest festival, Pentecost. Jesus' followers were in a room together. They heard a wind. They saw flames of fire.

They felt different: God was making them bold and strong to tell the news.

One of those who helped spread the news was Jesus' friend Simon Peter.

"Turn away from wrongdoing. Be baptized in the name of Jesus. God will forgive you. God is calling you to be his child."

Another was Paul. He journeyed many miles to many places telling the news.

"Since you are God's dear children," he said, "you must try to be like him. You must show love in your life, as Jesus did to all of us."